Adopting a Cat

by Isabel Thomas

Picking a cat

Are you thinking of getting a cat?
You can visit a pet shelter.

There are lots of cats in the shelter. They are waiting to be adopted.

All cats are different. Experts will help you pick the right cat.

They will tell you what you need.

Prep the house.

Get rid of toxic plants and dangling strings.

Put the litter box in a hidden corner.
Put it far from the food and water.

Bring a blanket when you visit the shelter. The cat can sniff it.

Bring the blanket when you collect the cat. The smell will help the cat to relax.

Settling in

To start, keep the cat in one room. Put the cat bed in there.

Be strict and keep exits shut.

Let the cat settle in.

Cats can feel timid to start with.
Let the cat come to you.

Cats like to sleep, groom and sniff.

Set up boxes in hidden spots.

Cats love puzzles and things to jump on.

You can scrunch up card scraps.

Soon the cat will feel relaxed. Then it can roam in the house.

Look Back

Encourage students to use the images to review the topic.